MAUI BEE BOOKS

MAUI BEE BOOKS

Printed by: CreateSpace
ISBN-13: 978-1-63028-006-2

PRINCESS ISABELLA

BY
KARLA BACKLUND

For All The Wonderful Grandkids

ILLUSTRATED BY CLAUDIA GADOTTI

When Princess Isabella
woke up, she
wanted a penguin.

Isabella wanted a penguin,
because she had been
dreaming of penguins.

The Princess had been dreaming of penguins
swimming and diving in the pool.

She had been dreaming of penguins playing
'catch me if you can' in the garden.

Princess Isabella had
been dreaming of
penguins playing
'hide and seek'
all throughout
her home, the Royal
Palace of Madrid.

She had been dreaming of penguins playing beautiful music in the concert hall.

She had been dreaming of penguins
cooking in the kitchen.

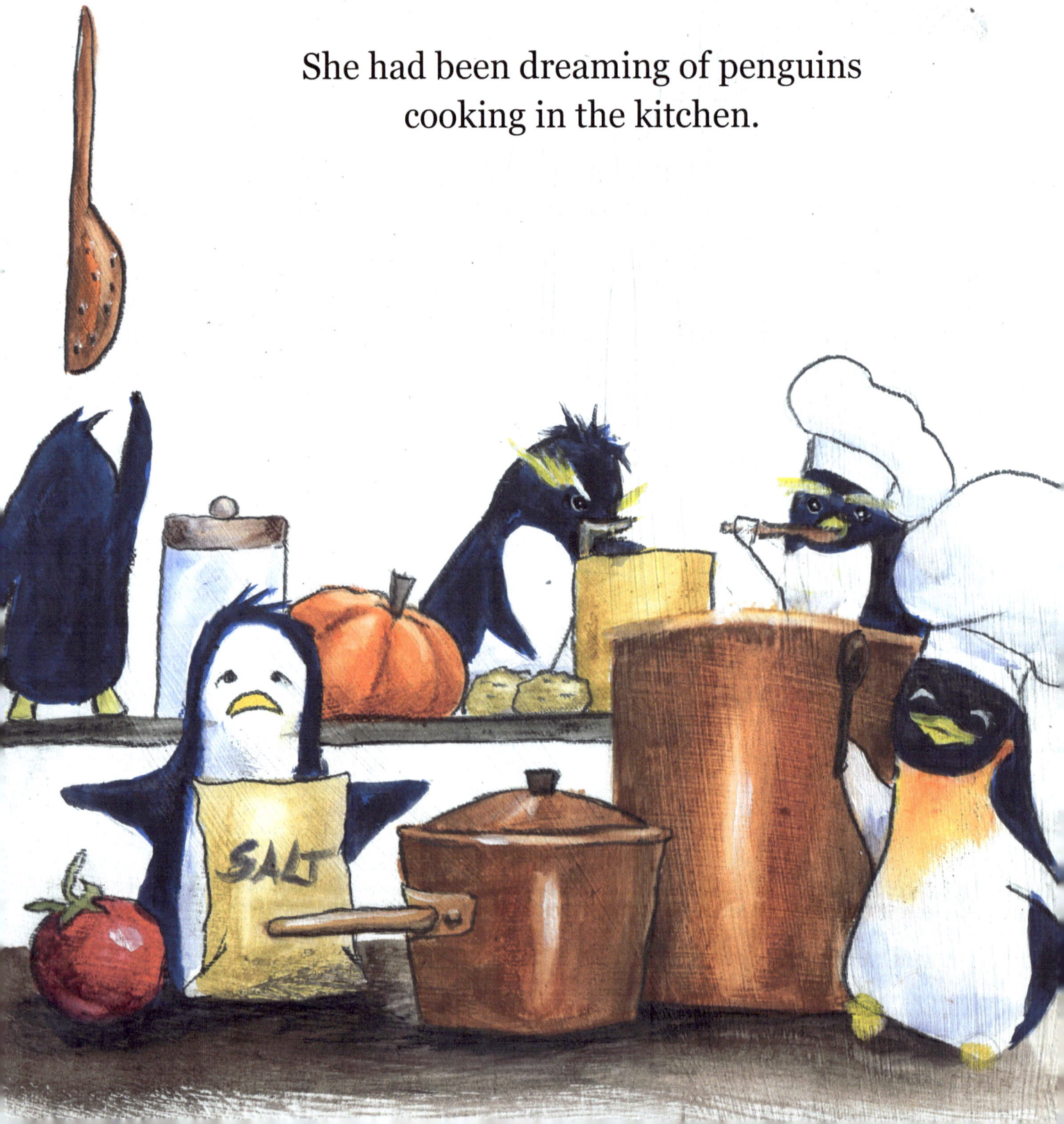

Isabella had dreamed of penguins, in her own little parlor, sharing tea and biscuits and telling stories of all their adventures.

Therefore, the very first thing
Princess Isabella said
to her dressing maid was,
"I would like a penguin, please."

"So sorry Miss Isabella, but
I don't know what a penguin is."
said the maid. She helped
Isabella get
dressed for breakfast.

When Isabella was
seated for breakfast, she said
to her serving maid,
"I would like a penguin, please."

The serving maid ran in a panic to the Royal Chef.
"Princess Isabella would like a penguin!".
"Here's some nice fresh watermelon and
strawberries instead." said the Chef.

When Princess Isabella was at her
lessons, she said to her Governess,
"I would like a penguin, please."
"Here's a book about penguins and some
drawing paper," said her Governess.
"You can read about penguins and paint
pictures of them." Isabella devoted
her morning, to reading about penguins
and painting pictures of her penguin dreams.

Princess Isabella had lunch with her mother, the Queen, and her grandmother, the Queen Mother. Isabella said to them, "I would like a penguin, please."

"She's so adorable," said her mother,
the Queen. "Such a delightful
imagination for a child,"
said her grandmother,
the Queen Mother.

In the afternoon, Princess Isabella
went to see her father, King Castilla,
the King of Spain. "I would like a
penguin, please, Father." said Isabella.
"A penguin!" exclaimed the King.
"And why in the world do you
want a penguin?"

So Isabella told her father her dream
and showed him her paintings.
The King laughed and laughed and for
a little while, he forgot all about the
problems and worries of the kingdom.

"Very well, Isabella,
you shall have your
penguins," promised the King.
"Oh Father, truly?!"
"Yes truly," said the King.
"When Father? When?"
"Very soon, Isabella. Every
morning when you wake up,
you should look for penguins."

As the King of Spain, King Castilla was used to solving some very complicated problems. So it did not take him long to find some extra-special penguins for Princess Isabella.

Every morning when Princess Isabella
woke up, she looked for penguins.
Finally, one morning, when she ran
to her balcony, she saw penguins
swimming and diving in the pool.

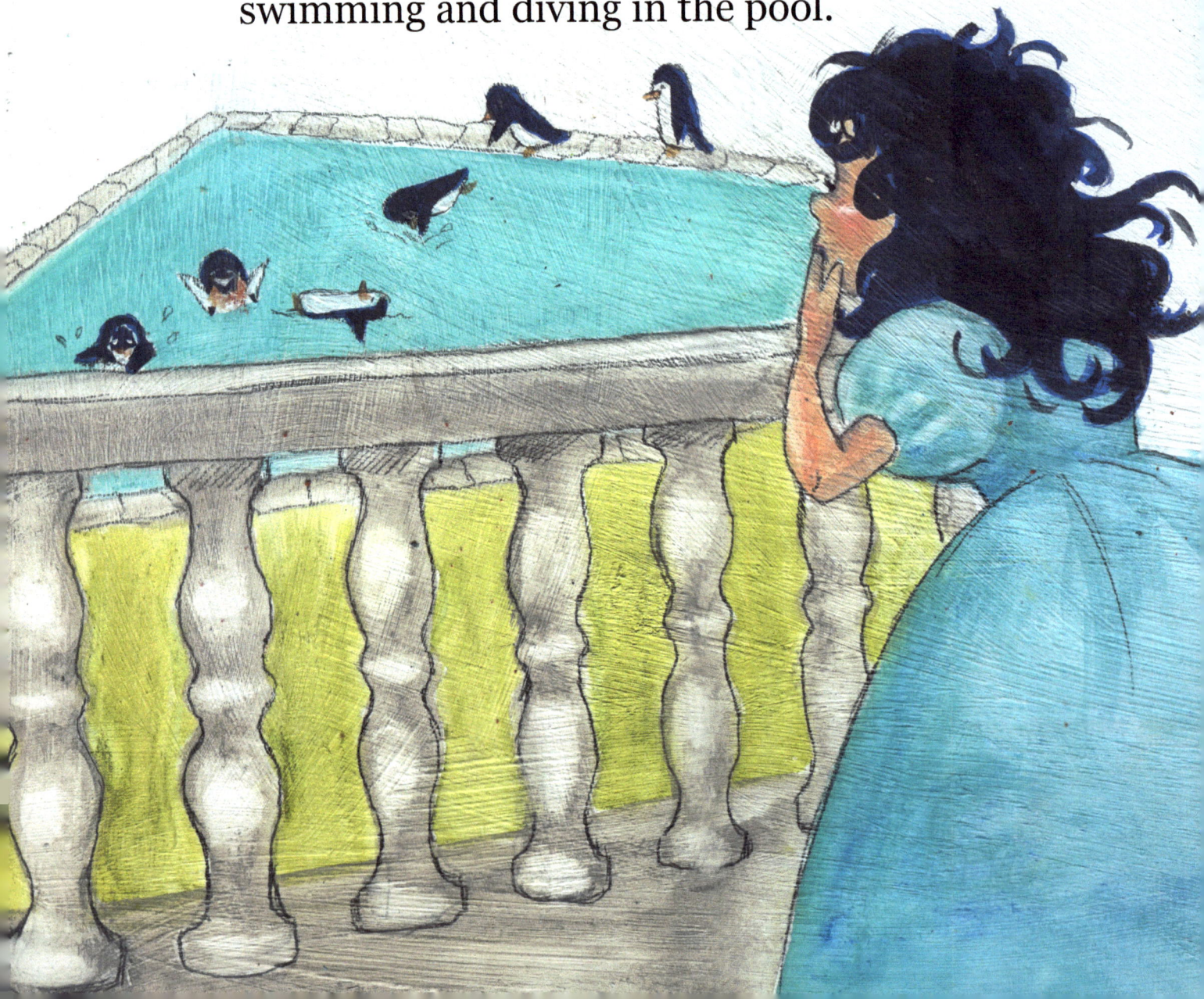

Isabella ran down to the
courtyard, where she found penguins
playing 'catch me if you can' in the garden.

She ran into the
great hall, and found
penguins playing
'hide and seek',
all throughout the
Royal Palace of Madrid.

Isabella ran to the kitchen, where she found penguins cooking breakfast. She ate a biscuit the penguins had made for her and proclaimed it "perfectly yummy"!

Princess Isabella ran to the concert hall, where she found penguins playing beautiful music. She danced with great joy all around the stage, while the penguins put on a royal performance.

Isabella was especially happy. She ran to her little parlor and there she found her father, King Castilla, the King of Spain, sharing tea and biscuits with several penguins.

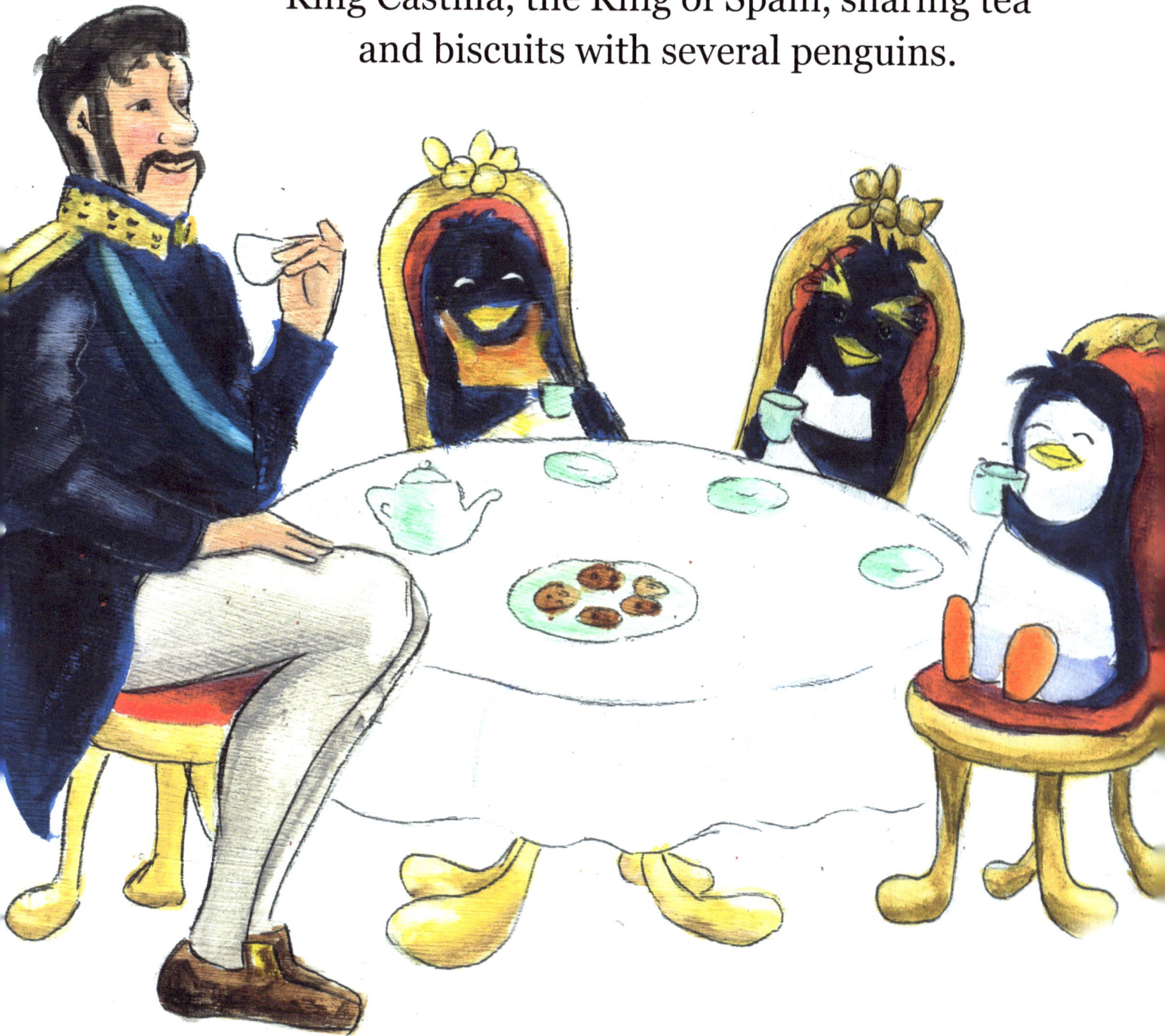

Isabella ran to her father and gave him a great big hug. "Thank you Father! Thank you for all the penguins and for making my dream come true."

So Princess Isabella and King Castilla had tea and biscuits with the penguins and listened to the marvelous stories of all their exciting adventures.

MAUI BEE BOOKS

www.ingramcontent.com/pod-product-compliance
Lightning Source LLC
Chambersburg PA
CBHW042115040426

42448CB00003B/277